MONTREAL CANADIENS

BY BRENDAN FLYNN

Book design by Maggie Villaume
Cover design by Maggie Villaume

Photographs ©: Kathy Willens/AP Images, cover; David Kirouac/Icon Sportswire, 4–5, 7, 29; Montreal Canadiens/Wikimedia, 8, 11; AP Images, 13, 15, 18–19, 23; IHA/Icon Sportswire, 17, 21, 25; Ed Betz/AP Images, 26–27

Press Box Books, an imprint of Press Room Editions.

ISBN
978-1-63494-493-9 (library bound)
978-1-63494-519-6 (paperback)
978-1-63494-570-7 (epub)
978-1-63494-545-5 (hosted ebook)

Library of Congress Control Number: 2022902272

Distributed by North Star Editions, Inc.
2297 Waters Drive
Mendota Heights, MN 55120
www.northstareditions.com

Printed in the United States of America
082022

ABOUT THE AUTHOR

Brendan Flynn is a San Francisco resident and an author of numerous children's books. In addition to writing about sports, Flynn also enjoys competing in triathlons, Scrabble tournaments, and chili cook-offs.

TABLE OF
CONTENTS

1

Rookie Cole Caufield scored four goals in the 2021 semifinal between the Montreal Canadiens and the Vegas Golden Knights.

BACK TO THE
FINAL

In spring 2021, the Montreal Canadiens were looking to snap a long drought. It had been 28 years since the team had last reached the Stanley Cup Final. The Canadiens barely even made the 2021 playoffs. But they upset their first two opponents. Then they faced the Vegas Golden Knights in the semifinal.

After five games, Montreal led the series three games to

two. Game 6 was a tense battle. The Canadiens took the lead twice. Vegas tied it back up twice. The game went to overtime tied 2–2.

Less than two minutes into the extra period, Vegas tried to seal the deal. But Montreal goalie Carey Price made two huge saves. Then the Canadiens pounced. Phillip Danault carried the puck over the Vegas blue line. Defenders raced over to stop him. So he flipped a pass to his left. Artturi Lehkonen was wide

HERE COME THE HABS!

In the city of Montreal, Quebec, many people speak both English and French. So it's no wonder the Canadiens have a French-language nickname. Fans call the team "the Habs." The name comes from *les habitants*. The phrase means French-speaking farmers living in Quebec.

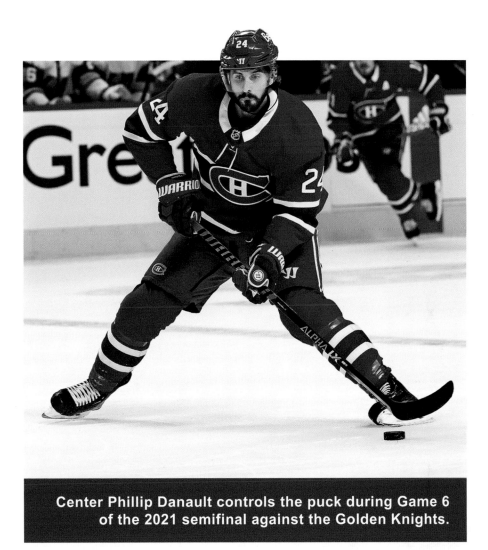

Center Phillip Danault controls the puck during Game 6 of the 2021 semifinal against the Golden Knights.

open. Lehkonen ripped a wrist shot into the net. For the first time since 1993, the Canadiens were headed to the Stanley Cup Final!

2

Didier Pitre was one of the Canadiens' first stars.

THE EARLY YEARS

*T*he Montreal Canadiens are the oldest team in the National Hockey League (NHL). In fact, the Canadiens are the only team that's been around longer than the league itself. They began playing in the National Hockey Association (NHA) in 1909. The NHL wasn't formed until 1917.

The Canadiens quickly became one of the best teams in hockey. In those early days, the Stanley Cup was a challenge cup. That meant teams from different leagues could challenge whoever held the trophy. The Canadiens won their first Stanley Cup in 1916. They defeated the Portland Rosebuds of the Pacific Coast Hockey Association.

That first championship team had a number of star players. Georges Vézina played goalie. He spent 16 years with the Canadiens. Today, the best goalie in the NHL each season receives the Vezina Trophy.

Newsy Lalonde led the Canadiens' offense. The high-scoring center once racked up nine goals in an NHA game. His best NHL game came in 1920 when he scored six times. As of 2021, that remained a team record. Lalonde also served as a player-coach from 1917 to 1921.

In 1924, the Canadiens won the NHL Final. Then they defeated the Calgary Tigers of the West Coast Hockey League (WCHL) to take the Stanley Cup. They won another NHL title the next year. But they lost the Cup to the Victoria Cougars of the WCHL.

Georges Vézina grew up in Chicoutimi, Quebec. His calmness in goal earned him the nickname "the Chicoutimi Cucumber."

Finally, in the 1926–27 season, the NHL took control of the Stanley Cup. The league's playoff champion would win the trophy and hold it for a year. The Canadiens were successful in that era, too. They won the Cup back-to-back in 1930 and 1931.

Hall of Fame center Howie Morenz was the superstar of those teams. Morenz had been a scoring machine since his first

HOWIE MORENZ

Howie Morenz played 12 of his 14 NHL seasons with the Canadiens. He was known for his daring one-man rushes against the defense. Morenz won the Hart Trophy as the league's most valuable player three times. Sadly, his career was cut short when he suffered a badly broken leg in 1937. Six weeks later, Morenz died of complications from the injury. In 1945, he became a member of the first class of the Hockey Hall of Fame.

Howie Morenz became a legend for his speed, physical play, and inventiveness on the ice.

pro season in 1924–25. He won the NHL scoring title twice. Morenz also scored an amazing 40 goals in 44 games in the 1929–30 season.

Meanwhile, George Hainsworth kept the opposing scorers in check. Hainsworth took over as goalie in 1926. He won the Vezina Trophy in each of his first three seasons.

The Canadiens went through a bit of a dry spell in the 1930s. But they came back to win the Stanley Cup again in 1944 and 1946. Some top scorers led the way. Elmer Lach and Buddy O'Connor held down the center position. And Toe Blake played left wing. The Canadiens also featured a fiery young right wing named Maurice Richard. He led the Habs to another Cup in 1953. That set the stage for one of the most dominant runs by any team in NHL history.

Elmer Lach hugs the Stanley Cup after winning the championship in 1953.

MAURICE RICHARD

Few athletes were more famous during the 1940s and 1950s than Maurice "Rocket" Richard. He joined the Canadiens as a 21-year-old forward in 1942. In his third year, he scored 50 goals in one season. He became the first NHL player to do so. Plus, he did it in just 50 games. It took 36 years before anyone matched that feat.

However, Richard was nearly as famous for his fists as he was for his scoring. Richard often ranked among the league leaders in penalty minutes. But Canadiens fans continued to root for Richard like no other player.

They had good reason. Richard was an All-Star for 14 straight seasons. He won eight Stanley Cups with the Canadiens. He retired in 1960 with 544 career goals. At the time, that was the league's all-time record.

Maurice Richard led the NHL in
goals five times.

3

Maurice Richard celebrates with the Cup after winning the 1958 Final.

DYNASTIES

Most teams would be thrilled with one stretch as the best team in the league. The Canadiens are one of the few teams in any sport that can count many dynasties in their past. Their first run began in the 1955–56 season.

Maurice Richard was one of many

Quebec natives and French Canadian stars on the team that season. High-flying center Jean Béliveau led the league with 47 goals. Bernie Geoffrion earned the nickname "Boom Boom" for his strong slap shot. And Richard's 19-year-old brother, Henri, made his NHL debut for Montreal that season.

The Canadiens won their eighth Stanley Cup in 1956. That was more than any team in the NHL. Then they left the

JACQUES PLANTE

Jacques Plante was a game changer in many ways. But he's probably best known for being the first goalie to wear a mask in a game. It happened in 1959. Coach Toe Blake wasn't happy about it. But then the Canadiens went on an 18-game unbeaten streak. Blake stopped his grumbling, and the mask was there to stay.

Jacques Plante started wearing a mask after a puck broke his nose during a 1959 game. He made the mask himself at home.

rest of the league in their dust by winning the next four in a row.

They got help along the way from defenseman Doug Harvey and goalie Jacques Plante. Harvey was a rock-steady defender for Montreal from 1947 to 1961. Plante won the Vezina Trophy six times between 1956 and 1962.

The Canadiens' second dynasty began in 1965. They won four Stanley Cups over the next five years. Béliveau, Henri Richard, and right wing Claude Provost were among the holdovers from the 1950s. They provided veteran leadership for the team's young talent. These stars included wingers Jacques Lemaire and Yvan Cournoyer. Serge Savard and Jacques Laperrière kept the defense strong.

In 1967, the NHL grew from six to twelve teams. The Canadiens won the first two Stanley Cups of the expansion era.

Serge Savard crashes into the St. Louis Blues' goalie as the winning goal scores during Game 4 of the 1968 Stanley Cup.

They added two more titles in 1971 and 1973. Then they steamrolled the league in the late 1970s. From 1976 to 1979, Montreal won four straight Cups.

The 1970s Canadiens were a dazzling collection of talent. Ken Dryden was the NHL's top goalie. He won five Vezina Trophies in his eight years with the Habs.

Savard, Guy Lapointe, and Larry Robinson were Hall of Fame defensemen.

Meanwhile, the Canadiens had plenty of elite scorers. Speedy right wing Guy Lafleur became the team's next French Canadian star. Lafleur scored at least 50 goals in each of six straight seasons. Left wing Steve Shutt was no slouch, either. Shutt led the NHL with 60 goals in 1976–77. And Bob Gainey was one of the game's great two-way forwards.

Over time, those stars began to retire. After that, Stanley Cup parades became less common in Montreal. But the Habs made a surprise title run in 1986. Forwards Mats Näslund and Guy Carbonneau led the way. Then, in 1993,

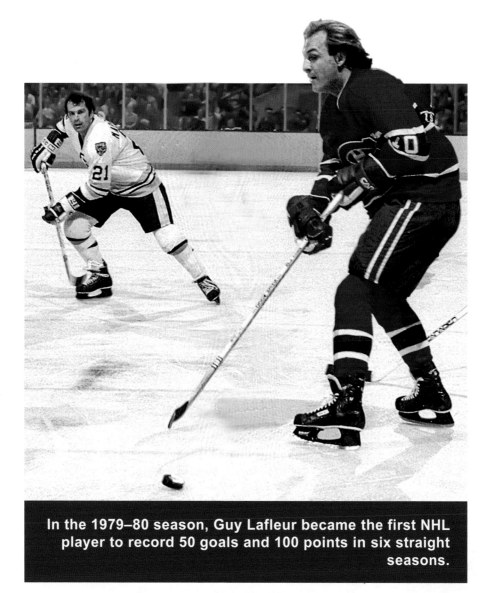

In the 1979–80 season, Guy Lafleur became the first NHL player to record 50 goals and 100 points in six straight seasons.

the Canadiens defeated Wayne Gretzky's Los Angeles Kings in the Stanley Cup Final. That marked the team's 24th Stanley Cup—by far the most in history.

4

Andrei Markov fights for the puck during a 2007 game.

BACK TO THE
FUTURE

After the 1993 Stanley Cup, the Canadiens struggled for years. But certain players made the team exciting to watch. Drafted in 1998, Andrei Markov became one of the rocks of the Canadiens. The two-way defenseman played all his 16 NHL seasons in Montreal.

In 2021, Montreal fans finally renewed their Stanley Cup hopes. However, the magic ran out in the Final. The Canadiens lost to the Tampa Bay Lightning in five games. Even so, the playoffs provided important experience for Montreal's next wave of prospects.

Twenty-one-year-old center Nick Suzuki led the team in the playoffs. He recorded seven goals and nine assists. He also scored an overtime game-winner during the playoffs.

COREY PERRY

Winger Corey Perry spent most of his long career with the Anaheim Ducks. But Perry joined the Canadiens in late 2020. At age 35, he was brought in to provide leadership. Montreal got its money's worth. Perry's only year with the Canadiens ended with a Stanley Cup Final appearance.

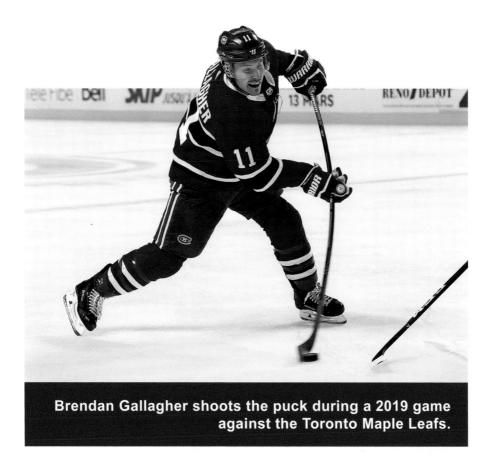

Brendan Gallagher shoots the puck during a 2019 game against the Toronto Maple Leafs.

Veteran forwards Josh Anderson and Brendan Gallagher provided offensive support. Defensemen Jeff Petry and Shea Weber also played key roles. And Carey Price provided his usual strong play in goal. Canadiens fans hoped the next dynasty was just around the corner.

MONTREAL CANADIENS
QUICK STATS

FOUNDED: 1909

STANLEY CUP CHAMPIONSHIPS: 24 (1916, 1924, 1930, 1931, 1944, 1946, 1953, 1956, 1957, 1958, 1959, 1960, 1965, 1966, 1968, 1969, 1971, 1973, 1976, 1977, 1978, 1979, 1986, 1993)

KEY COACHES:

• Dick Irvin (1940–55): 431 wins, 313 losses, 152 ties

• Toe Blake (1955–68): 500 wins, 255 losses, 159 ties

• Scotty Bowman (1971–79): 419 wins, 110 losses, 105 ties

HOME ARENA: Bell Centre (Montreal, QC)

MOST CAREER POINTS: Guy Lafleur (1,246)

MOST CAREER GOALS: Maurice Richard (544)

MOST CAREER ASSISTS: Guy Lafleur (728)

MOST CAREER SHUTOUTS: George Hainsworth (75)

Stats are accurate through the 2020–21 season.

GLOSSARY

CENTER
A forward who typically plays in the middle of the offensive zone.

DYNASTY
A team that has an extended period of success, usually winning multiple championships in the process.

EXPANSION
The way leagues grow by adding new teams.

PLAYOFFS
A set of games to decide a league's champion.

PROSPECT
A player that people expect to do well at a higher level.

SLAP SHOT
A shot in which a player winds up and slaps the puck with great force.

TWO-WAY
Skilled at both offensive and defensive play.

VETERAN
A player who has spent several years in a league.

TO LEARN
MORE

BOOKS

Doeden, Matt. *G.O.A.T. Hockey Teams*. Minneapolis: Lerner Publications, 2021.

Nicks, Erin. *NHL*. Minneapolis: Abdo Publishing, 2021.

Omoth, Tyler. *A Superfan's Guide to Pro Hockey Teams*. North Mankato, MN: Capstone Press, 2018.

MORE INFORMATION

To learn more about the Montreal Canadiens, go to **pressboxbooks.com/AllAccess**.

These links are routinely monitored and updated to provide the most current information available.

INDEX